Compiled by Joan Frey Boytim

EASY SONGS FOR THE BEGINNING BARITONE/BASS

Laura Ward, *pianist*
Larry Rock, *engineer*
Recorded May 2000, Settlement Music School, Germantown, Pennsylvania

ISBN: 978-0-634-01972-2

G. SCHIRMER, Inc.

DISTRIBUTED BY

HAL•LEONARD®
CORPORATION

7777 W. BLUEMOUND RD. P.O. BOX 13819 MILWAUKEE, WI 53213

To access companion recorded
piano accompaniments online, visit:
www.halleonard.com/mylibrary
Enter Code
6476-0136-1264-5559

T0048531

PREFACE

Easy Songs for Beginning Singers will appeal to the middle school age group as well as to many beginning high school, college, and adult students. There are between 22 and 24 songs in each book with online accompaniments included.

Suitable vocal repertoire for the middle school student taking voice lessons has been rather sparse. For many years, most young people did not begin vocal study until the ninth or tenth grade level or even later. There was a misconception that it was a dangerous practice to study voice at an earlier age. As teachers have become more knowledgeable, as students are maturing much earlier, and as musicals are being produced in the middle schools, one finds many young people beginning lessons in the seventh and eighth grades and even earlier.

The foreign language texts have been purposely eliminated to make the songs very easy to learn. Modification has been made to the dated English versions and, in some cases, new texts have been provided. The songs are quite short and they generally have rather moderate tessituras. The maximum ranges, explored in only a few selections, are C to G for soprano, A to E for mezzo, C to F-sharp for tenor, and A-flat to E-flat for baritone. Most songs do not use those extended ranges.

A number of the songs will not be familiar but should prove to be a welcome addition to well known repertoire published in these collections. At the same time, I have included a few popular standards in each volume. Songs in the female books explore many folk songs and interesting translated French bergerettes and early German lieder. The male volumes each contain a number of English and American folksongs, spirituals, and several art songs. There are several quite humorous songs in each of the books.

Most of the accompaniments are suitable for student pianists. A few songs in each volume will be more of a challenge to lead the student directly into Schirmer's *First Book of Solos* and *First Book of Solos Part II*.

Birth and death dates for composers have been included whenever possible. These dates are simply not known for a few of the composers, particularly minor musical figures who had few published works. In lieu of birth and death dates, publication dates are provided, when known, to allow a teacher or student at least some chronological perspective for a song.

It is my hope that these four volumes will provide a new and worthwhile source of music for the novice singer of any age, as well as a fun collection for the more experienced student of voice.

Joan Frey Boytim

BIOGRAPHY

Compiler Joan Frey Boytim is a nationally recognized expert in teaching beginning voice students and has conducted workshops, seminars, and master classes across the United States. She is the compiler of the widely used series *The First Book of Solos*, *The First Book of Solos Part II*, *The Second Book of Solos*, and *The First Book of Broadway Solos*.

CONTENTS

The price of this publication includes access to companion recorded piano accompaniments online, for download or streaming, using the unique code found on the title page. Visit **www.halleonard.com/mylibrary** and enter the access code.

Aura Lee

W.W. Fosdick

George R. Poulton
published 1861

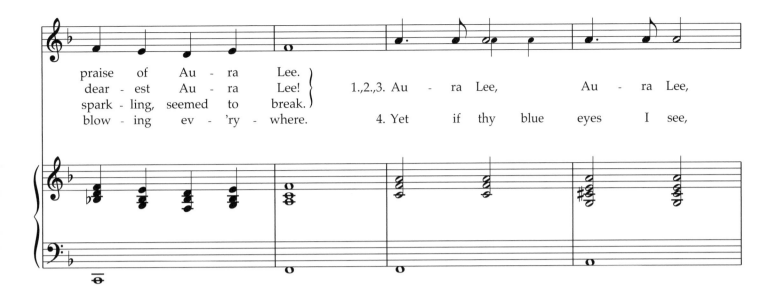

praise of Au - ra Lee.
dear - est Au - ra Lee!
spark - ling, seemed to break.
blow - ing ev - 'ry - where.

1.,2.,3. Au - ra Lee, Au - ra Lee,
4. Yet if thy blue eyes I see,

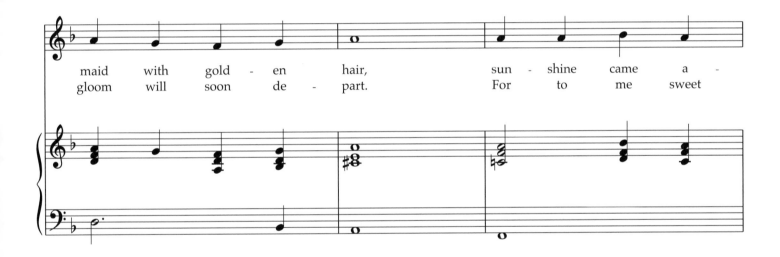

maid with gold - en hair,
gloom will soon de - part.

sun - shine came a -
For to me sweet

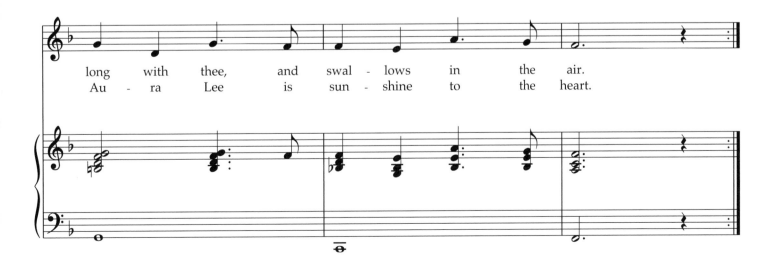

long with thee, and swal - lows in the air.
Au - ra Lee is sun - shine to the heart.

Beautiful Dreamer

text by the composer

Stephen C. Foster
1826-1864

Beau - ti - ful dream - er,
Beau - ti - ful dream - er,

wake un - to me;
out in the sea

star - light and dew - drops are wait - ing for
mer - maids are chaunt - ing the wild lor - e

thee. _____
lei. _____

Sounds of the rude world
O - ver the stream - let

heard in the day, lulled by the moon-light have all passed a-
va-pors are borne, wait-ing to fade at the bright com-ing

way. _____ Beau-ti-ful dream-er,
morn. _____ Beau-ti-ful dream-er,

queen of my song, list while I woo thee with
beam on my heart, e'en as the morn on with the

soft mel-o-dy. Gone are the cares of
stream-let and sea; then will all clouds of

10

Funiculi, Funicula

English text by
Edward Oxenford

Luigi Denza
1846-1922

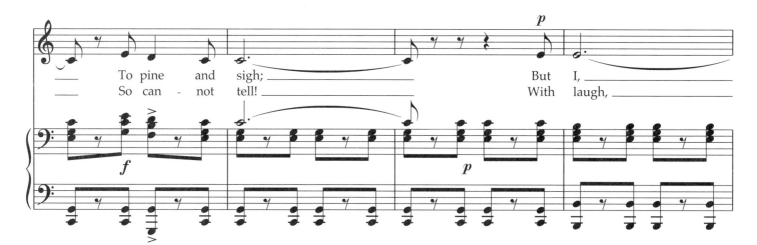

To pine and sigh; _____ But I, _____
So can - not tell! _____ With laugh, _____

I love to spend my time in sing - ing _____ Some joy - ous
with dance and song the day soon pass - es, _____ Full soon is

song; _____ Some joy - ous song; _____ To
gone: _____ Full soon is gone; _____ For

set _____ the air with mu - sic brave - ly ring - ing _____
mirth _____ was made for joy - ous lads and lass - es _____

The Erie Canal

New York work song, ca. 1820

Foolish Questions

American folksong
arranged by Benjamin M. Culli
b. 1975

Go Down, Moses

African-American spiritual
arranged by Benjamin M. Culli
b. 1975

When Is - rael was in E - gypt's land,
spoke the Lord, bold Mo - ses said,
foes shall not be - fore you stand,

Let my peo - ple go, Op - pressed so hard they
Let my peo - ple go, If not so I'll smite your
Let my peo - ple go, And you'll pos - sess fair

could not stand, / first born dead, / Ca - naan's land, Let my peo - ple go.

Go down, Mo - ses, Way down in

E - gypt land, Tell old Pha - raoh To

let my peo - ple go. Thus let my peo - ple go. / Your

I Wish I Was Single Again

J.C. Beckel
published 1871

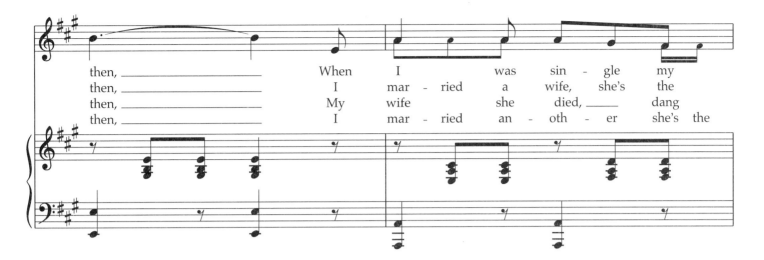

then, _____ When I was sin-gle my
then, _____ I mar-ried a wife, she's the
then, _____ My wife she died, _____ dang
then, _____ I mar-ried an-oth-er she's the

pock - ets did jin - gle, And I wish I was sin - gle a -
plague of my life, _____ I _____ wish I was sin - gle a -
lit - tle cared I, _____ To _____ think I was sin - gle a -
Dev - il's step - moth - er And I wish I was sin - gle

gain. _____
gain. _____
gain. _____
gain. _____

1. 2. 3.

4.

I
My
I

If You Were the Only Girl in the World

Clifford Grey

Nat D. Ayer
1887-1952

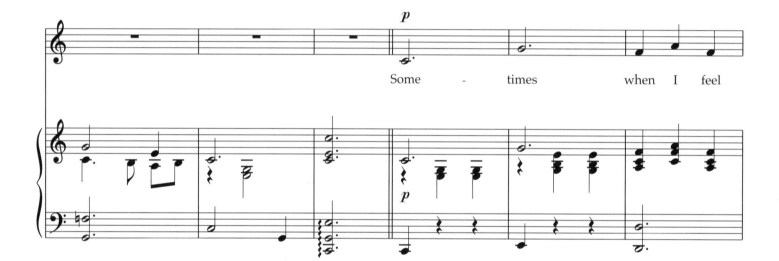

Some - times when I feel

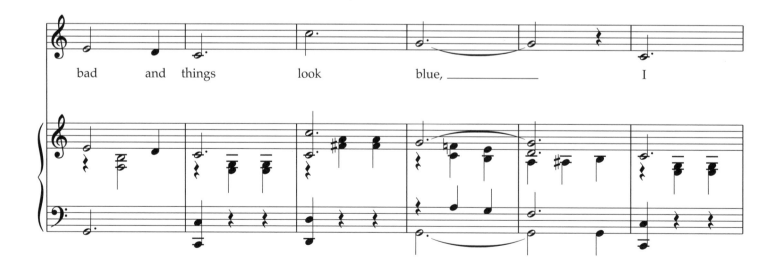

bad and things look blue, _____ I

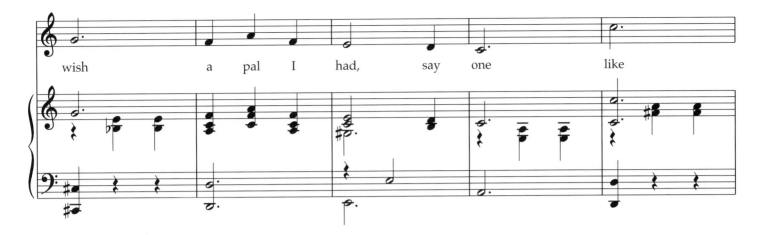

wish a pal I had, say one like

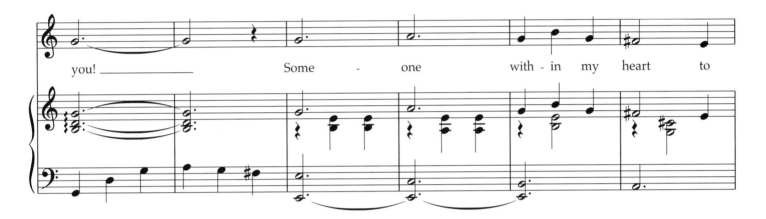

you! Some - one with - in my heart to

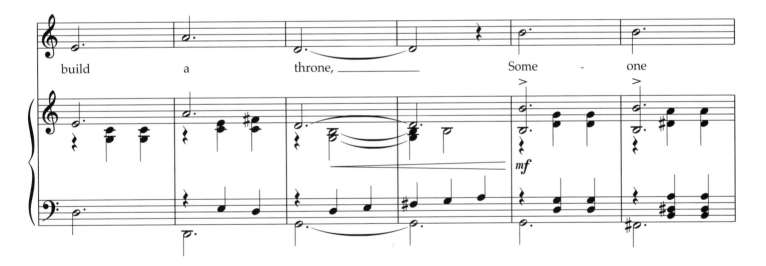

build a throne, Some - one

mf

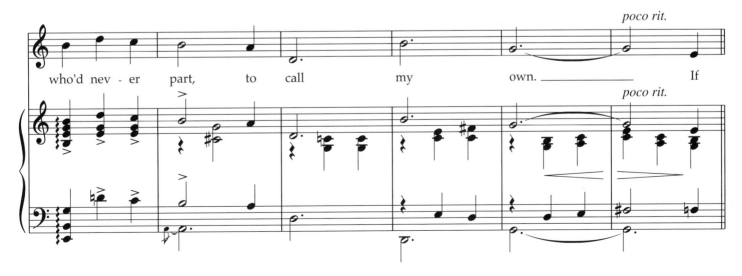

poco rit.

who'd nev - er part, to call my own. If

poco rit.

you were the on - ly girl in the world, And I were the

on - ly boy, _____ Noth - ing else would mat - ter in the

world to - day, We could go on lov - ing in the same old

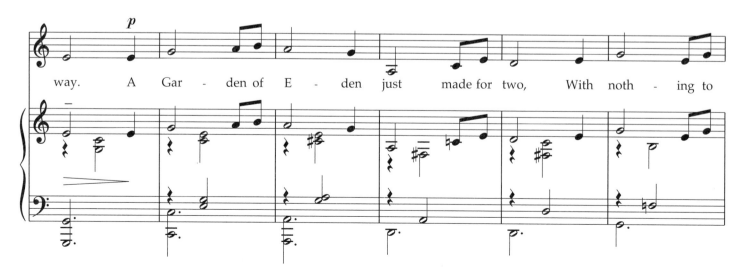

way. A Gar - den of E - den just made for two, With noth - ing to

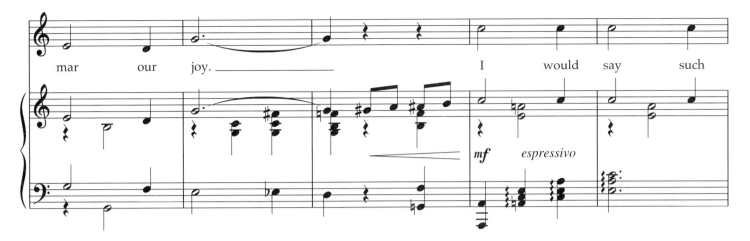

mar our joy. _____ I would say such

won-der-ful things to you, There would be such won-der-ful things to

do, If you were the on - ly girl in the world And

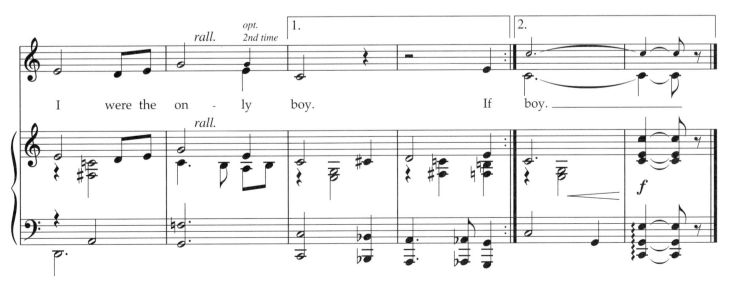

I were the on - ly boy. If boy. _____

The Lost Chord

Adelaide A. Procter

Arthur Sullivan
1842-1900

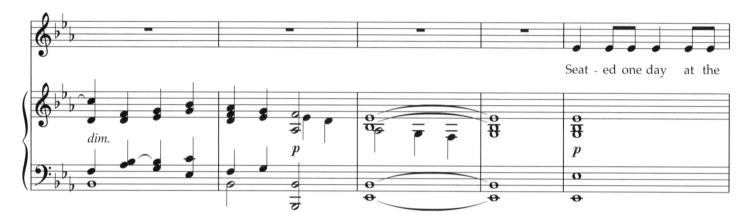

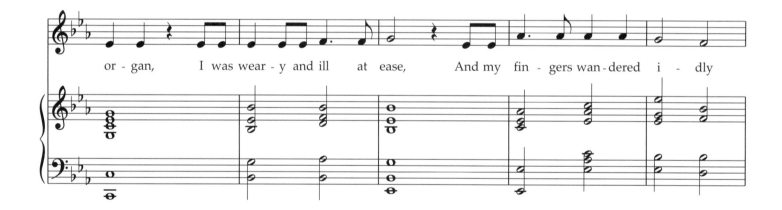

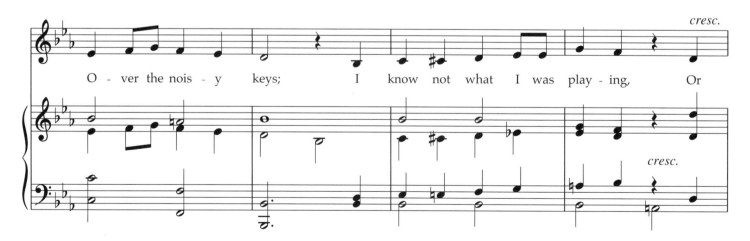

Seat - ed one day at the or - gan, I was wear - y and ill at ease, And my fin - gers wan - dered i - dly O - ver the nois - y keys; I know not what I was play - ing, Or

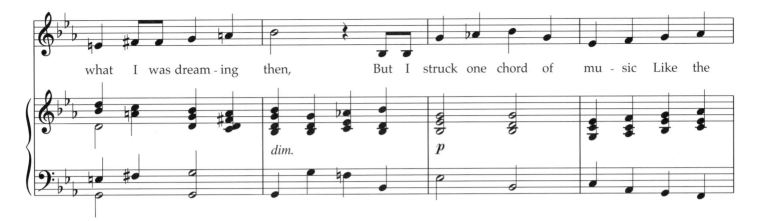

what I was dream-ing then, But I struck one chord of mu-sic Like the

sound of a great A - men, like the sound of a great _____ A -

men. It

flood-ed the crim-son twi-light Like the close of an an - gel's Psalm, And it

lay on my fe - vered spir - it With a touch of __ in - fin - ite calm;   It

qui - et - ed pain and sor - row Like love o - ver - com - ing strife,   It

seemed the har - mo - nious e - cho From our dis - cord - ant life.   It

linked all per-plex - ed mean - ings, In - to one per - fect peace,   And

trem-bled a-way in-to si - lence, As if it were loath to cease. I have

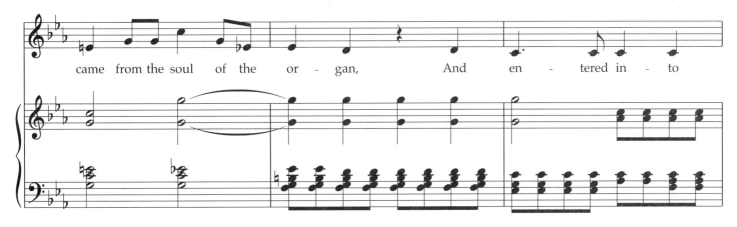

sought, but I seek it vain - ly, That one lost chord di - vine, Which

came from the soul of the or - gan, And en - tered in - to mine. It may be, that Death's bright an - gel Will

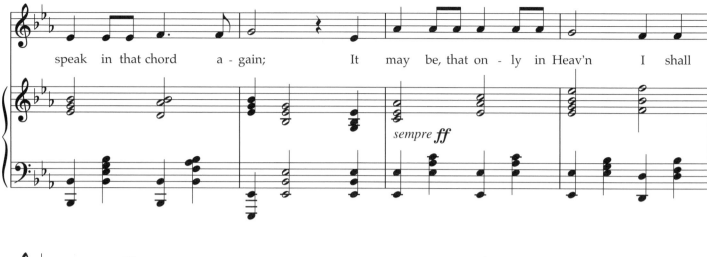

speak in that chord a - gain; It may be, that on - ly in Heav'n I shall

sempre **ff**

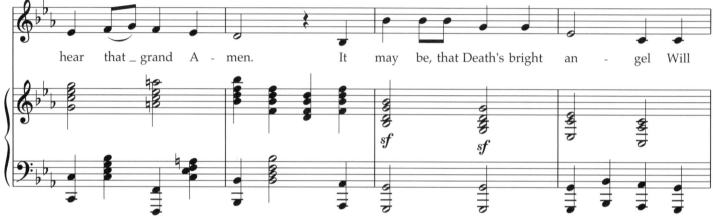

hear that _ grand A - men. It may be, that Death's bright an - gel Will

sf *sf*

ff *rit.* *con gran forza*

speak in that chord a - gain, It may be, that on - ly in Heav'n I shall

rit.

opt.

fff

colla voce con gran forza

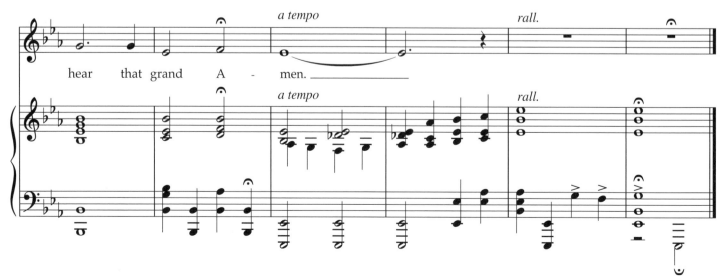

a tempo *rall.*

hear that grand A - men. _____

a tempo *rall.*

This page is blank to facilitate page turns.

The Jolly Miller

English, early 18th century
arranged by Charles Fonteyn Manney
1872-1951

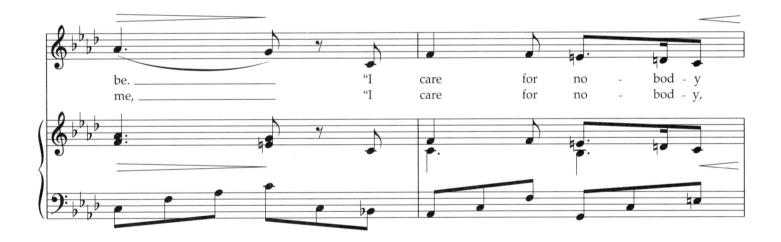

Joshua Fit the Battle of Jericho

African-American spiritual
arranged by Cynthia Jackson

down. You may talk a-bout your King of Gid-e-on, you may

talk a-bout your man of Saul, there's none like good old

Josh-ua at the bat-tle of Jer-i-cho. Up to the walls of

Jer-i-cho ___ he marched with spear in hand. "Go

blow them ram - horns," Josh - u - a cried, _ " 'cause the bat - tle is in my

hand." Then the lamb ram sheep horns be - gin to blow, _ the

trum - pets be - gin for to sound, Lord, old Josh - ua com - mand - ed the

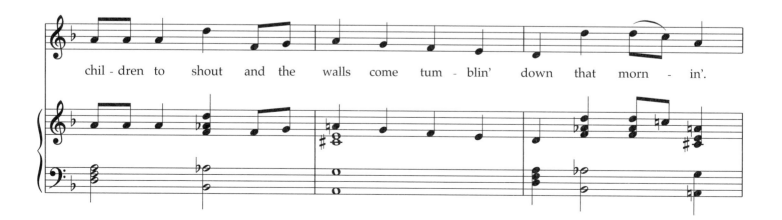

chil - dren to shout and the walls come tum - blin' down that morn - in'.

Josh - ua fit the bat - tle of ___ Jer - i - cho, ___ Jer - i - cho, ___

Jer - i - cho, _____ Lord, ___ Josh - ua fit the bat - tle of ___

Jer - i - cho ___ and the walls come tum - bl - in' down!

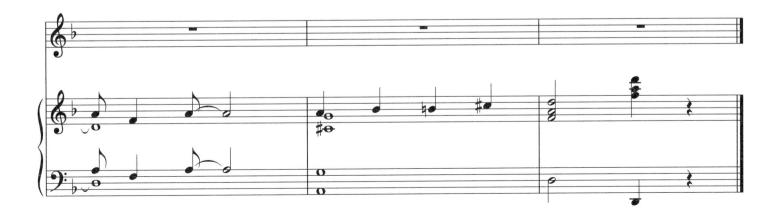

The Lark in the Morn

English folksong
arranged by Cecil J. Sharp
1859-1924

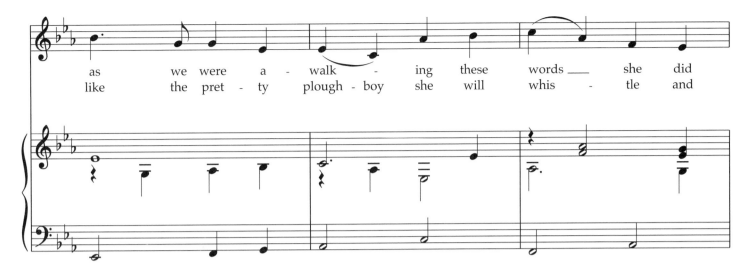

as / we were a-walk - ing these words ___ she did
like / the pret - ty plough-boy she will whis - tle and

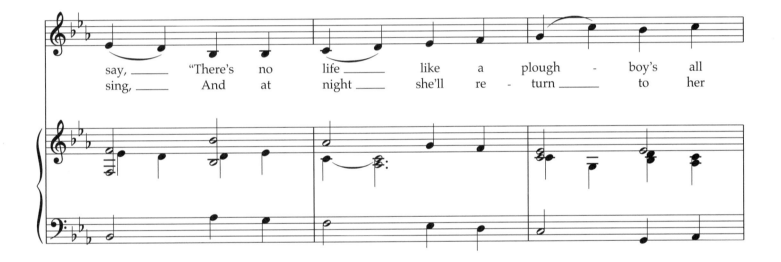

say, ___ "There's no life ___ like a plough - boy's all
sing, ___ And at night ___ she'll re - turn ___ to her

in the month of May."
own nest back a - gain.

The Minstrel Boy

Thomas Moore

traditional Irish melody
arranged by Jean-Baptiste Weckerlin
1821-1910

wild   harp slung _____ be - hind _____ him.
tore   its chords _____ a - sun - der; And

"Land of song," said the war-rior bard, "Tho' all the world be - trays _____ thee, One
said, "No chains shall _ sul - ly thee, Thou soul of love and bra - ver - y! Thy

sword at least _ thy _ rights shall guard, One _____
tones were made _ for the pure and free, They shall

faith - ful harp _____ shall praise _____ thee."
nev - er sound _____ in sla - ver - y!"

Mrs. Murphy's Chowder

traditional Irish-American
arranged by Benjamin M. Culli
b. 1975

man-y to be found; Silk hats, door mats, bed slats, dem-o-crats, co-co bells, door bells

beck-on you to dine; Meat balls, fish balls, moth balls, can-non balls,

come on in, the chow - der's fine.

Won't you chow - der's fine.

Smick, Smack, Smuck

John Philip Sousa

John Philip Sousa
1854-1932

I loved a maid long years a - go, A weird - er girl no one can show, She
I kissed her till her lips were raw, And then I tack - led to her jaw, Says
We kept it up for mor'n a week, Un - til her teeth came through her cheek, And

had a wart up - on her nose, And eyes that looked just like a crow's, She
I, "I want to breathe, my dear," She on - ly looked and wagged her ear, I
then she faint - ed right a - way, And nev - er winked the live - long day, I

had a fail - ing, I must say, 'Twas to be kiss - ing all the day, She'd
told her that I guess I'd stop, Says she, "My an - gel don't let up," A
felt so sad I near - ly died To think her mouth was four feet wide, I

kiss at morn, she'd kiss at noon, She'd kiss from Ju - ly up to June.
weird - er girl I nev - er saw, Say what you would, she'd ask for more.
took her to a doc - tor - shop, And soon he had her cheek glued up.

(See spoken lyrics)*

Spoken Lyrics
(monologue between each verse and the chorus)

1. Of course when I first formed her acquaintance, she was everything that was
   nice, so bashful and retiring, but on my asking leave of her after my third
   visit, as I held her hand at the door, she gazed wistfully with her languid,
   hungry eyes into my face, and holding her face temptingly, tremblingly
   near me, murmured, "Well you may – Just one, no more. " The blood rushed to
   my face, and in the nervousness of the moment I murmured, "I don't know how."
   "Oh! you Silly Goose, then I'll tell you."
   Chorus

2. I was growing faint, and told her it was becoming painful – "What? Painful!
   the easiest thing in the world – Just... "
   Chorus

3. Then I fled in terror from that remarkable female, but no peace do I know, for
   the horrors of that terrible experience haunt me day and night. Ever and anon
   a large pair of hungry, languid eyes start up before me and murmur...
   Chorus

*Pause the recording for the monologues. The return to the chorus is anticipated on the recording by the addition of two
pick-up notes.*

Chorus

Face to face, and nose to nose, Smick, Smack, Smuck, and a - way she goes;

Lay her eye - brow on your col - lar, Hug her so that she can't hol - ler,

Tell her that you're al - ways true, Squeeze her 'til her face turns blue,

Keep it up for fif - teen hours, __ Then be - gin a - new.

Out of My Soul's Great Sadness

(Aus meinen grossen Schmerzen)

Heinrich Heine
English text by
Frederic Field Bullard

Robert Franz
1815-1892

This song has no introduction; one has been added for this edition.

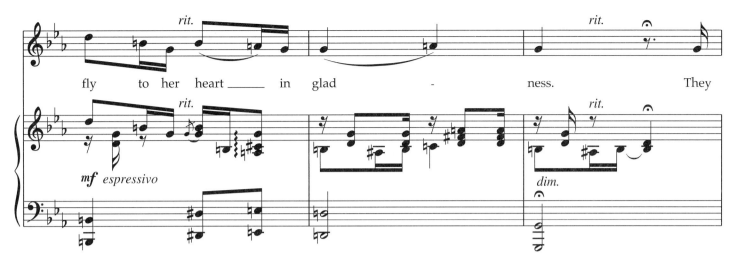

fly to her heart _____ in glad - ness. They

found her, and round her hov - ered, And now they've come back, and they

scold me, And yet not a song - let has told _____ me What

they in her heart dis - cov - ered.

Request

(Bitte)

Nikolaus Lenau
English text by
Joan Boytim

Robert Franz
1815-1892

Larghetto sostenuto

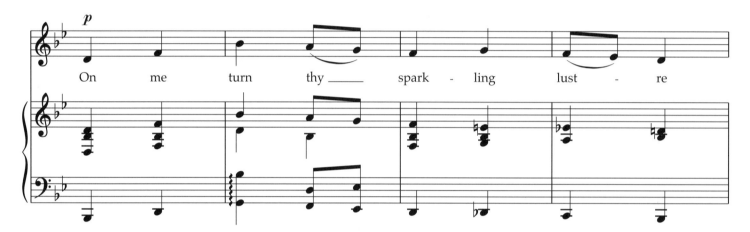

On me turn thy _____ spark - ling lust - re

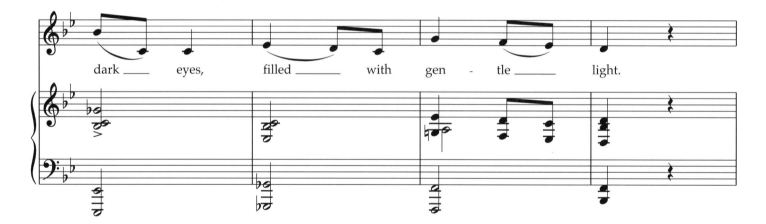

dark _____ eyes, filled _____ with gen - tle _____ light.

Ear - nest, mild, with _____ dream light beam - ing

fair as ____ day, and calm as ____ night.

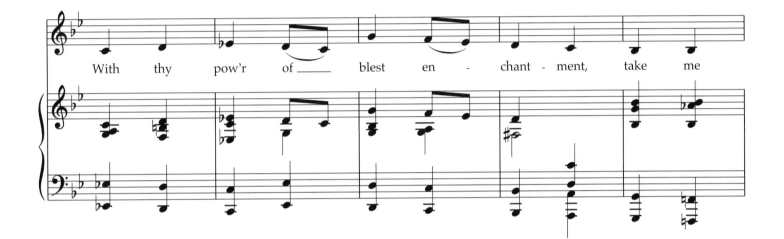

With thy pow'r of ____ blest en - chant - ment, take me

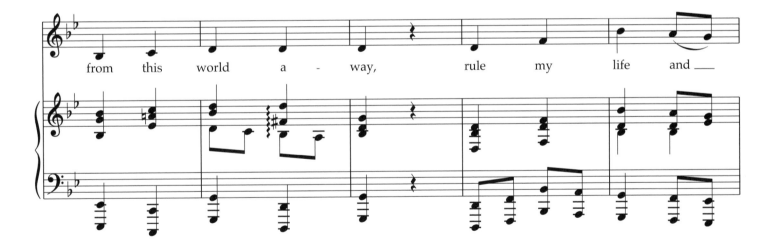

from this world a - way, rule my life and ___

rule for - ev - er. Thee _ a - lone ___ will I o - bey.

dim.

Simple Gifts

traditional Shaker song

'Tis a gift to be sim-ple, 'tis a

gift to be free, 'tis a gift to come down

where you ought to be, and when we find our-selves in the

place just right, 'twill be in the val - ley of

love and de - light. When true sim - plic - i - ty is gained, to

bow and to bend we ___ won't be a - shamed. To turn, turn will

be our de - light till by turn - ing and turn - ing we come out right.

Sometimes I Feel Like a Motherless Child

African-American spiritual
arranged by Harry T. Burleigh
1866-1949

long ways ___ from home, _____ a

rit.   *a tempo*

long ways ___ from home. _____ A

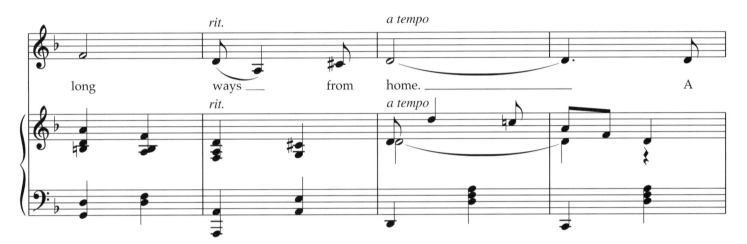

long ways ___ from home, _____ a

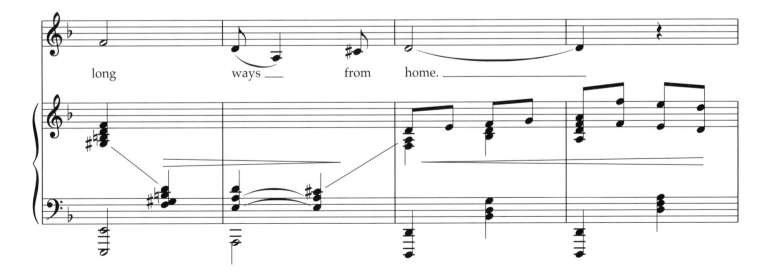

long ways ___ from home. _____

ways __ from home, _____ a long ways __ from

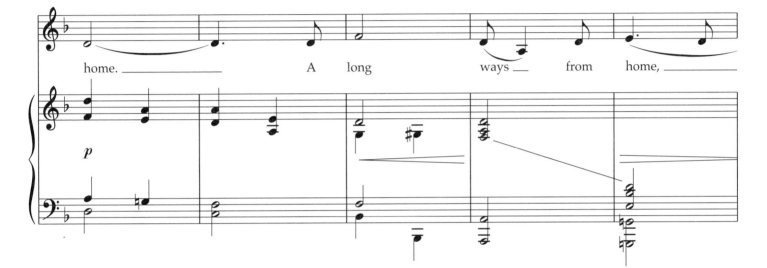

home. _____ A long ways __ from home, _____

rit. e dim. *a tempo*

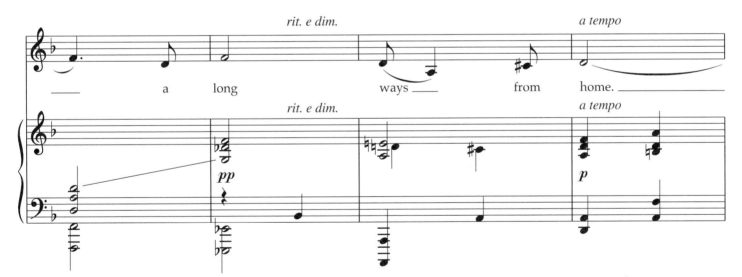

__ a long ways __ from home. _____

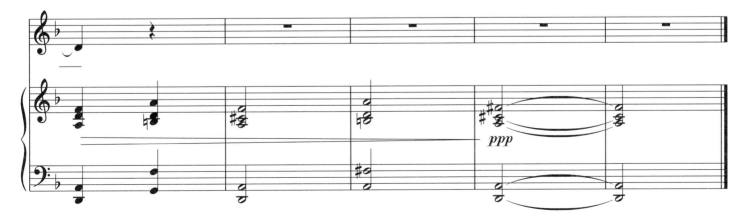

The Story of a Tack

J.A. Parks
published 1896

There was a

boy, there was a tack, There was a teach - er

new. The tack sat down up - on its head, The

teach-er sat down, A-las, the teach-er sat down too.

* Then, straight-way, and with some abruptness he a-rose; He leaped into the air with a piercing cry! __ The

p *colla voce*

air grew chilly, and the blood within each trem-bling young-ster froze, For

deep, dark, ruddy gore was in his eye! He seized the boy, who

a tempo

a tempo

mf

* Sung freely on indicated pitches

trem - bling stood, And shook in ev - 'ry

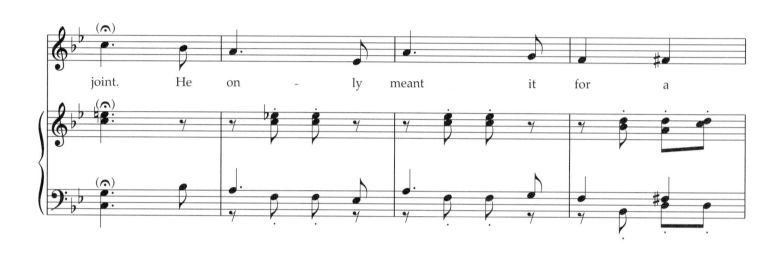

joint. He on - ly meant it for a

joke, But the teach - er, some-how, He some - how failed to

see the point of the tack!

Where Did You Get That Hat?

text by the author

Joseph J. Sullivan

published 1888

prop - er - ty and mon - ey. And when the will it was read out, they
out the slight - est rea - son. If I go to a "chow - der club," to
said too long we'd tar - ried. So off to church we went right quick, de -

told me straight and flat; If I would have his mon - ey, I must al - ways wear his hat!
have a jol - ly spree; There's some - one in the par - ty, who is sure to shout at me:
ter - mined to get wed. I had not long been in there, when the par - son said to me:

Where did you get that hat? Where did you get that tile?

Swing Low, Sweet Chariot

African-American spiritual
arranged by Cynthia Jackson

With movement

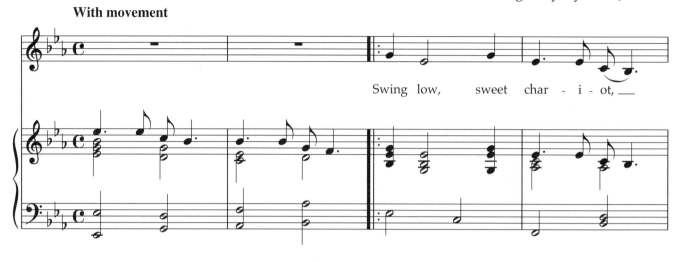

Swing low, sweet char - i - ot, ___

com - in' for to car - ry me home. Swing low, sweet char - i - ot, ___

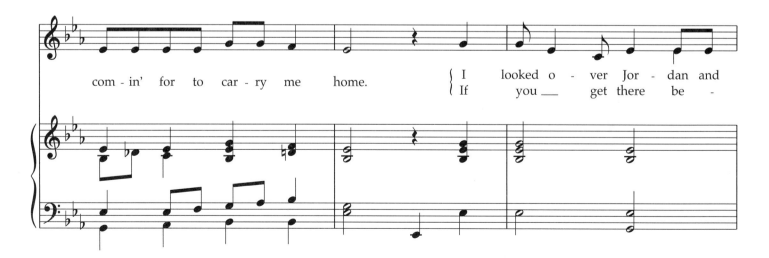

com - in' for to car - ry me home.
I looked o - ver Jor - dan and
If you ___ get there be -

While Strolling Through the Park One Day

words and music by Ed Haley
and Robert A. Keiser*

Lightly

mf

While __ stroll - ing through the park one day

in the mer - ry month of May I was tak - en by sur - prise by a

pair of ro - guish eyes. In a mo - ment my poor heart was stole a - way. _____ A

*pseudonym for Robert A. King (1862-1932)

smile was all she gave to me. Of

course, we were as hap-py as can be. Ah! I im-

me - di-ate - ly raised my hat and fi - nal-ly she re - marked. I

nev - er shall for-get that love-ly af - ter-noon I met her at the foun-tain in the park.

You'll Miss Lots of Fun When You're Married

Edward M. Taber

John Philip Sousa
1854-1932

Valzer grazioso

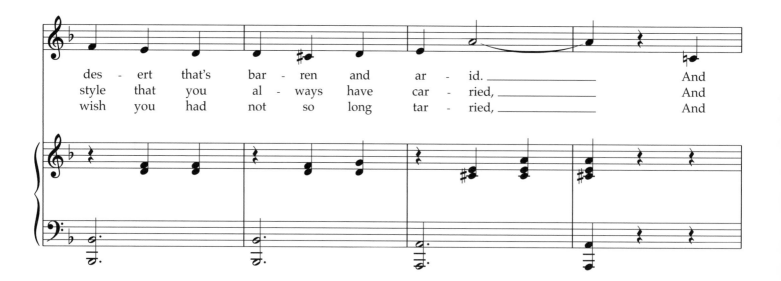

des - ert that's bar - ren and ar - id. _____ And
style that you al - ways have car - ried, _____ And
wish you had not so long tar - ried, _____ And

I would ad - vise him a part - ner to seek. *Spoken:* { *Still,* You'll
think with re - morse on your old reck - less ways. { *Nevertheless,* You'll
then. I sup - pose you will vil - li - fy me. { *But, all the same,* You'll

pp

miss lots of fun when you're mar - ried.
miss lots of fun when you're mar - ried.
miss lots of fun when you're mar - ried.